Little Book of Autumn

Book 7 of the Little Book Series
A poetry collection by Claire Buss

Other works by Claire Buss:

The Gaia Collection
The Gaia Effect
The Gaia Project
The Gaia Solution
The Gaia Collection (all 3 books together)

The Roshaven Books
The Rose Thief
The Interspecies Poker Tournament – The Roshaven Case Files No. 27
Ye Olde Magick Shoppe

Poetry
Little Book of Verse, Book 1 of the Little Book Series
Little Book of Spring, Book 2 of the Little Book Series
Little Book of Summer, Book 3 of the Little Book Series
Spooky Little Book, Book 4 of the Little Book Series
Little Book of Winter, Book 5 of the Little Book Series
Little Book of Love, Book 6 of the Little Book Series
Little Book of Autumn, Book 7 of the Little Book Series

Short Story Collections
Tales from Suburbia
Tales from the Seaside
The Blue Serpent & other tales
Flashing Here and There

Anthologies
Underground Scratchings, Tales from the Underground anthology
Patient Data, The Quantum Soul anthology
A Badger Christmas Carol, The Sparkly Badgers' Christmas Anthology
Dress Like An Animal, Haunted The Sparkly Badgers' Halloween Anthology
The Last Pirate, Tales from the Pirate's Cove anthology

Little Book of Autumn

Book 7 of the Little Book Series

Apple Pie
Back to School
Brain Fog
Bread Week
Chilli Inna Bowl
Colour Changes
Crisps
Crunchy Leaves
Dwindling Light
Falling Into Fall
Firework
Harvest Festival
Hibernating Hedgehog
Mellow Yellow
Oooh Cup of Tea
Pumpkin Spice
Season of Mists
Sense of an Ending
Sometimes
The Bonfire
The New New Year
The Scent of Autumn
Weather Morph
Will It Snow
Words Words Words

Apple Pie

I baked an apple pie today
I don't know why

I had to go and buy things I don't usually keep
around

Special apples and pre-rolled pastry
It feels like cheating but

I never bake, I rarely cook, I can devour with the
best

Something inside me screamed out
I want pie, bring me pie, make pie

So I peeled and I cored and I chopped and I rolled

It's autumn I figured, the time of great harvest
A pie is just the thing we need

Now comes the big question

To serve it with cream or with custard or ice cream
Maybe yogurt or crème fraiche or a splash of milk

Back to School

The summer holidays have been grand
We've done nearly everything planned
The sun has shone and the rain came down
I've mostly turned round each frown
We've visited family and seen good friends
At times it felt like holidays would never end
We went to the beach and swam in the sea
We walked past lots of flowers and counted the bees
A hike to visit the castle ruins up on the hill
And we've definitely eaten our entire fill
Of Greggs sausage rolls and Happy Meals
Not a big fan but he had all the feels
And now it's the night before the best day so far
We're going back to school, we're raising the bar
It's a brand new year, new teacher, new class
I'm hoping he doesn't give them too much sass
I'm excited he's going but I know I'll be sad
Hoping naively I don't miss him too bad
I feel sure home time will soon come around
And he'll chatter excitedly in the playground
So let's raise our mugs in an exhausted cheer
They go back to school, it's finally here!

Brain Fog

I'm looking at a screen
Words are lurking
Somewhere
I can't process my thoughts
A fog invades
Vision is cloudy and slow
I rub my eyes but the motion is slurred
I blink heavily
So tired
Brain is not firing
Cylinders are blocked or broken or cold
I came here to do something but...
... the memory is lost in the ether
I write but the words skitter
I try to post but get halfway before I'm lost
It's too late for yawns
A haze comes down
A mist
A fog
Unable to collect these thoughts dancing in my
head
Just out of reach of my fingertips

Bread Week

A slice of toast in the midst of school run madness
A quick jam sandwich for hungry kids
A chip butty with melted butter and ketchup
A mop-up tool for stew - that's the greatness of bread

It comes in brown, multigrain and white
50/50, honeyed oat, gluten-free, rye
Brioche, fruit, cheesy, crusty, soft as a cloud
Practically every combination possibly

A quick breakfast, a lazy brunch
A grabbed snack, a double-decker doorstep
A melty mid-afternoon pick me up
A cheap yet tasty bean covered tea

You can't beat the humble loaf
It comes in every variety
Comforting and delicious
It's why we have an extra slice

Chilli Inna Bowl

On a chilly autumn evening
When you're looking for some comfort
And your hungry tummy is calling
It's time for chilli inna bowl

Everyone has their own recipe
Different kinda meats, more or less veg
But all agree on the need for kidney beans
Essential for chilli inna bowl

Make it vegan, make it veggie
Put in five types of bean
Coriander, sweetcorn even chocolate
It all works for chilli inna bowl

Serve it with rice, with jacket potatoes
Over chips or hot dogs inna roll
Add sourcream and cheese
Enjoy that chilli inna bowl

Colour Changes

It's not time yet but it soon will be
The mornings will reclaim some shadows
And the evenings will lengthen
A darkness is coming

It's still yellows and oranges
Bright things still twinkling
Cerulean blue dancing in the sky
Summer still shines

But the seasons will shift
September rustles around the corner
And Autumn is checking
That it's dancing shoes are ready

Browns and reds and purples are shifting
Greens and blues and yellows fading
The earth is saving is strength
Changing colours, falling

Crisps

I love crisps
I love the crunch and the munch
I love the rustle of the packet
and that salty nomnomnom

Me and crisps go way back
Back when they used to come with a little salt pack
Back when cheese & onion used to be green
and salt & vinegar used to be blue

These days there are so many flavours
In can be hard to choose what to munch
And now that I'm dairy-free
I have to read alllllllll the ingredients

A crisp sandwich is still a fun guilty pleasure
And dipping crisps in food or with pate
They go with every filling
Perfect for every snack occasion

I just try not to note the fat content
Especially in the share bag I didn't share
Or the tube of Pringles I hid behind the microwave
until the kids had gone to bed

Crisps can be shared
But they're more likely to make you mean
As you hold the packet possessively
And lick your fingers after each dip

Yeah me and crisps are good mates
We see each other nearly every day
I just can't seem to leave them alone
Maybe tomorrow I'll...

... ooooh is that a new flavour?

Crunchy Leaves

I loved the way the floor crunches when I walked
The rustle of the leaves
And the scrunch scrunch munch

I used to kick in abandon when I was just a child
I never considered what might be hidden in those
leaf piles
A hedgehog, a smelly poop, broken glass

Leaping into leaf piles used to be the best thing
ever
Now that I'm a parent it's the worst thing in the
world
I cannot go with that free spirit abandon

Too scared of the crunch
Too scared of what's beneath
Lost my scrunchy fun

So leaves, keep falling for me, making piles of joy
One day perhaps I'll lose my growed up
And then I'll leap and jump and crunch

Dwindling Light

It's getting dark now Mummy
The sun has gone to bed early
The birds aren't singing anymore
And the clouds are grim and scary

It's getting cold now Mummy
I don't want to wear shorts anymore
I need a new rain jacket and wellies
Else there will be puddles on the floor

It's very windy out there Mummy
It's whipping all the leaves and trees
It doesn't seem to have a problem
Blowing through me with ease

It's so very rainy now Mummy
Drizzly and damp all day long
There comes the regular deluge
Like it was summoned by a song

The trees look so very bare now Mummy
They lost all their leaves
Do you think they need a hat or scarf?
I don't want them to freeze

It's getting dark now Mummy
In the morning and before the night
I want an extra cuddle please
I want to hug you extra tight

Falling Into Fall

September yawned and we all fell in
The evenings grew longer and darker
And winter blew from afar, chilling the weather
The sun decided to rest a while
And cardigans were pulled from bottom drawers
Autumn is upon us, marching on regardless
We spent too long on the beach
And tripped over our buckets and spades
Now we fall into hot chocolates and fingerless
gloves
The start of a new year of school and learning
Shiny shoes and smart uniforms
Brand new lunchboxes
All the little children falling into lessons
With not too much grumbling…
We're falling out of love with salads
And plumping for pies, stews and roasts
Not forgetting crumble and custard
Falling into bad habits of curling up on the sofa
No more early morning runs
And one more biscuit from the tin
Fireworks, bonfires, sticky toffee apples
Crunchy leaves and rain, pumpkin spice everything
We're falling into fall

Firework

They crash and bang in the darkened sky
Like heralds of an ancient power
The crowds beneath them gasp in awe
Then start chatting between them
A firework only holds the attention for a short while

Despite the fizz, the whizz and the bang
Eventually all the sounds and all the smells
All the colours and all the sky glitter
Just start looking the same
It's another firework, let's go get a hot chocolate

The ones at the beach are best
They shoot out over the surf
The fear of standing on the beach in pitch black
With just fake stars exploding overhead
And a shore of strangers sharing the moment

At the end no-one claps
There's a murmur of disappointment that this is
the finish
The lights have fizzled out and the camaraderie
lost
We all file out, some pushing, some shoving
The cars packing the road in the rush to leave

A sadness then that the display is over
A regret that you didn't pay full attention
But when you live at the beach
You have to remember
It goes on from October through to November

Harvest Festival

All things bright and beautiful
all tins and packets gathered in

All things wide and wonderful
nothing perishable please

It's time for the Harvest Festival
Time to gather everything we've sown

Whilst bringing the crops in may not be so
The bounty of autumn beginning is here

The perfect time to give thanks
To look back, review and re-set

Did everything you plant in Spring grow?
Has Summer helped to bake your plans?

This harvest-time what can you use now?
What can you blend into something new?

Often at time of plenty, a time of glut
Make sure you bottle and can and preserve

Don't let a single drop go to waste
But take the time to celebrate your bounty

Remember the collection for school
The scrabbling in the back of the cupboard

Using up those old tins and packets and jars
Giving them freely to others

There's nothing to say no school, no collection
Go gather your harvest and spread your joy

Hibernating Hedgehogs

The hedgehogs are fading
Leaving the British countryside
Endangered
Misunderstood
Unloved
They are receding into memory and myth
Leave a saucer of milk out for the hedgehog
They say
But milk will make them poorly
They're better off with worms
And slugs and snails
Make your garden hodgeheg friendly
A wood pile for the hibernate
Be wary disturbing compost and leaves
For hedgehogs like to nestle deep within
They sleep through winter
All curled up in their little spiny balls
But they'll eat the vermin from your garden
Spring through Autumn

Mellow Yellow

The hot burn of summer is melting into a golden
glow
The heat is banking, pockets here and there
The sun is still sparkling on the water, still shining
in the sky
But this brightness is losing its intensity
Exhaling with a relaxed sigh
Before it turns too cold and dark and wintery
Luxuriating in the mellow yellow of autumn
The whole earth resting

Mellow in light, in music, in ambiance and style
Laid back and relaxed and zen in its being
Warm tones and spices and the peeking of
pumpkins
Lattes, crumbles, mochas and strudel
Oranges, purples and deep reds take over
Earthy warm brown treacle hushes nature
A deep breath in and then waiting but not
impatiently
The serenity of time taken

Oooh Cup of Tea

Ooooh cup of tea
Is that one for me?
I really need one right now

Ooooh cup of tea
Pop it on my knee
I promise not to spill it

Ooooh cup of tea
You heard my plea
I'm gasping for some refreshment

Ooooh cup of tea
It's necessary you see
One of 'those' days

Ooooh cup of tea
I've only had three
And that's since this morning

Ooooh cup of tea
Milk first is the key
I don't care what anyone says

Ooooh cup of tea
I'll pay any fee
If you just keep 'em coming

Pumpkin Spice

Pumpkin spice latte? Pumpkin spice latte?
What rubbish is this on my menu?
I just came in for a coffee you see
Just a cup of hot lava to wake up my senses
Not dull them with spices of pumpkin

How do you spice a pumpkin anyway?
I always thought they were a sort of roasting
vegetable
I never really gave eating them much thought
We had one in art class once
Waited till it had moulded before we drew its
corpse

I hear that it's not pumpkin at all but a mixture of
other things
Seems sneaky to me to label a thing one but for it
to be another
Sign of the times we live in I suppose
And it comes as a latte which is basically warm
milk
Where's the coffee to be found in one of those?

But this is just the tip of the iceberg
This imaginary spice is everywhere
You can buy it in candles and desserts and
milkshakes
In ice creams and puddings and lipsticks of all
things
It doesn't even really exist!

I just want a coffee
I'm not being funny
Don't get me started on the point of a flat white
I don't want oat milk or soya or coconut
But make sure you give me six sugars with that!

Seasons of Mist

Rolling in off the sea, curling over the pavements
Smothering the ground with swirling cloud
Tis the season of mists and fogs and hazes
Autumn has landed

Blurry shapes and dimly lit lamps
Orange headlights burbling through
A cold frost round the edges in those early morns
A sense of disquiet, of the unknown

Traffic mists and water mists
Mists that cling to forests and woods
Secret animal meeting mists and rustling of leaves
mists
Mists that burn slowly, reluctantly away

The misty twilight has a different power
It speaks of fairys and gnomes and such
For if you dance in the mushroom ring then
You'll be lost in the fall mists for ever

Sense of an Ending

When the nights draw in
And the cold nips your nose
There is the sense of an ending

When the leaves fall to the floor
And conkers litter your path
There is the sense of an ending

When the flowers fade away
And the earth stays brown and closed
There is the sense of an ending

When jumpers and cardigans come out
And the dresses and shorts go away
There is the sense of an ending

When salads and ice cubes
Are replaced for stews and hot chocolate
There is the sense of an ending

When the long lazy hazy days of summer roll close
And the drawn-out nights of fog and damp arrive
There is the sense of an ending

Goodbye Summer
Hello Autumn
From all ends comes a new beginning

Sometimes

Sometimes the words flow and the meaning is clear
Other times it's a fight to the death as one syllable wrestles another for freedom

Sometimes ideas spark continuously after each other like brilliant fireworks exploding in your mind
Other times the blank canvas fills the room silently screaming

Sometimes characters can't stop yammering and time passes till suddenly thousands of words have appeared
Other times...

Sometimes the world is full of colour and light with creativity shooting out of every pore
Other times despair is blacker than black and its cold in the dark, all alone

Sometimes the rollercoaster becomes the merry-go-round and you are shouting to get off the ride
Other times you crave excitement in the dull minutiae

The Bonfire

By day the bonfire pile is nothing special
Bits of dry wood and broken furniture
All piled on
Sometimes it's a neat cone
Other times a heap that rises up
But at night
When the sky is dark and the stars are peeping
Then the bonfire holds its own

With flames licking wood hungrily
Leaping for the stars
Smoke billowing, cracking and creaking inside
With a pop and a frisson of sparks
Don't stand too close
Best to ring the bonfire with coats and gloves on
Clutching mugs of hot chocolate
Or chilli inna bowl

It rages for hours
The wood smell of its pyre
Permeating hair and clothes
When the fire gods finally tire of their offering
The flames die down
And the core heats on
Embers glowing long into the night
Remembering the joy as they leapt high

The New New Year

September is the new New Year
And I'll tell you for why
Although a time children may fear
Their parents just can't lie
Lockdown's been tough
Homeschooling's been rough
By July we'd all had enough
Back to school kid, with love

A new New Year means lots of new things
Costing an arm and a leg
Bedecking our children out like kings
Adhering to scholastic rules and regs
Shoes and coats they don't love
Ten packs of pencils, still not enough
Obnoxious coloured uniform is rough
Sorry kiddo, no choice, just tough

See the parents are filled with secret glee
Cos they'll have time for hot cups of tea
And space without noise, clutter or fuss
Or even, if they want, hours of hush
Lockdown's been tough
Homeschooling's been rough
By July we'd all had enough
Back to school kid, with love

The Scent of Autumn

A crisp apple, a baked pie
Cinnamon and ginger and mixed spice float by
Hot chocolates, hot toddys, plenty of germs

It's in the crisp leaf, the shiny conker
The squirrels who forage desperately
The birds who grow quiet

There's a smell of decay, of mushrooms, of death
But there's also a cleansing, a whiff of the frost
Cold white mornings with underfeet crunch

It's the sharpness in the nose and the prickle of
the eye
The need for gloves and hats and scarves
Numb toes stamping in boots

But no snow on the horizon
Fireworks night is especially nippy
Because everyone is out to see fake stars light up
the sky

Halloween on the other hand is usually trippy
Trick and treats litter the pavements
We dress up to forget, to pretend, to hide

I smell an ending but also a beginning
The start of the freeze, the clenching of the earth
Harvest time is over, it's time to live on our
gatherings

Have you showered love and light on your family?
Can you keep them warm through the long night?

Weather Morph

Bright blue skies and a shiny hot sun
Time to hit the beach and have fun, fun, fun
But the weather doesn't hold for long
And it's soon time to sing a new song

The heat of summer morphs to fog
The perfect weather to take a jog
There's mist and coolness all around
Leaves litter the entire ground

From sweat rolling down your nose
To trainers and socks on your toes
Time to find the hidden brolly
Go without at your own folly

Gone are the hazy lazy days
Now time for misty foggy ways
Heavy thunderstorms and muggy clouds
No congregating beach crowds

The weather has morphed from summer to fall
It's all happened in no time at all
We pack away our summer bodies
Preparing for endless hot toddies

For now it will be wet and cold
Pre-empting Winter taking hold
We'll snuggle down and take a breather
Maybe this autumn will be easier

Will It Snow?

Will it snow in November? I ask my mum and dad
No don't be silly, it's not cold enough for that

Will the sun shine hot instead then I wonder
But it seems that is something else not to ponder

November will rain and the leaves will fall
Apart from the fireworks there's nothing exciting at all

We can't put up the decorations for Christmas for weeks
And the cold wind continues to bite at our cheeks

Walking to school in the cold and the dark
The wind blows too much to play in the park

Instead we just sit and sip our hot drinks
Dreaming of snow and skating at the rinks

Are you sure it won't snow I ask one more time
Now, now my dear, please don't whine

I go to the window and look out at the lake
Then I gasp, and I peer, was that? Could it be? A flake?

Words Words Words

Why do we like words so much?
It's something we can't even touch
But we love to use them every day
In every unique and different way

So many ways to say hello and goodbye
Ask hundreds of questions, find out why
Chat to parents, speak to your mates
Keep on talking till it gets late

Use social media to spread them afar
Don't need to keep any in a jar
Just when you think you're going to run out
You'll find some new ones with plenty of clout

Let them tumble around in your head
Think about them while lying in bed
Try a few out, tap a few keys
Use them whenever you please

Your words are yours, they're just for you
Recycle old ones, create something new
A word here, a few more there
Words, words, words - everywhere!

~ENDS~

Collect all the seasonal Little Books and don't forget to add Spooky Little Book to your poetry collection today. Little Book of Christmas releases Winter 2020.

Spooky Little Book is a collection of Halloween-themed poetry celebrating everything spine-tingling and scary. Hide behind the sofa, watch out for the monsters under the bed and stock up on candy – you're going to need it!

Spooky Little Book is available on Amazon in both print and eBook – mybook.to/LBSPOOK

Poem from Spooky Little Book:

Bats

A dark shape swoops across the sky
Too fast to see
Its prey has no chance
Snatched out of the air

Living together in hidden caves
Hanging upside-down
Roosting and guarding their lairs
With delicate skin wings stretched over bone

Protected, venerated, a little bit feared
Superb predators
Unique communicators
They probably hoard gold

Yes
Bats are furry dragons of the night

About the Author

Claire Buss is a science fiction, fantasy & contemporary writer based in the UK. She wanted to be Lois Lane when she grew up but work experience at her local paper was eye-opening. Instead, Claire went on to work in a variety of admin roles for over a decade but never felt quite at home. An avid reader, baker and Pinterest addict Claire won second place in the Barking and Dagenham Pen to Print writing competition in 2015 setting her writing career in motion. She used to write prolific poetry and has recently returned to the rhyming couplet, enjoying herself immensely.

Sign up to Claire's newsletter for exclusive content and all the latest writing news: http://eepurl.com/c93M2L

Follow Claire on Twitter: @grasshopper2407

Like Claire on Facebook: facebook.com/busswriter

Visit her website: www.clairebuss.co.uk

Short Story Collections

Tales from Suburbia is a collection of short stories, plays and blog posts that intermingle my own personal experiences as a mum, the peccadillos of suburbia and the perils of social media! The subject matter varies from social observation to the humorous reflection of toddler life. Burying my Baby is heart-breaking. One Two, Cha Cha Cha is hilarious. This collection is full of human foibles and folly and is both amusing and empathetic.

> *"A wonderful, eclectic collection of stories."*
> *"This book is a box of chocolate in book form."*
> *"A varied collection of funny and touching stories and essay."*

You can buy *Tales from Suburbia* from Amazon in audio, print and eBook – mybook.to/talessub

Tales from the Seaside is a humorous collection of short stories reflecting on life by the seaside, attempts to successfully wrangle two small children and the result of being inspired by the sun, the sand and the sea. The perfect beach read; it will have you chuckling in your deckchair.

> *"These little tales are a delight to read."*
> *"A slice of life, perfectly captured."*
> *"Thought provoking yet easy to read, Buss achieves a perfect balance."*

You can buy *Tales from the Seaside* from Amazon in audio, print and eBook –
mybook.to/seasidetales

Printed in Great Britain
by Amazon